Everyday Vitamin Water Recipes

Nancy Bellamy

DEDICATION

To my beloved mother, I couldn't have done it without your support and encouragement to chase my dreams. My colleagues at the Lizarazu's Restaurant in Paris who supported me as I started my culinary career. My dear friend Jane, I thank you for being the best food taster in the world and assisting in my wacky food experiments.

DISCLAIMER

TABLE OF CONTENTS

PART 1

Health Guide

WHAT IS NATURAL VITAMIN WATER?

S oft drinks, or any processed beverages for that matter, are not a viable substitute for plain water. Even though 99% of the people are familiar with the fact that sugar-laced beverages are bad for their health, they still can't resist drinking them to quench their thirst. They cannot be blamed, for these beverages taste wonderful.

The taste is what lures people to these unhealthy beverages and soon they find it hard to let go of the habit. Well, if it's taste you are looking for and you cannot bear to gulp down any more plain water, there is a perfectly good alternative available to you: natural vitamin water. Vitamin water is healthy, reliable and has no side effects. Moreover, it can help you lose weight and sustain your body weight at a normal level.

Plain Water Is Boring ....

At its core, vitamin water is simply plain water to which you add fruits, vegetables and herbs. Not only does this remove the 'unhealthiness' of processed beverages but also ensures you don't spend any more of your hard-earned money on drinks that will ultimately destroy your health. No longer do you have to rely on pop to relieve your thirst.

A distinct advantage of homemade vitamin water is that there is virtually no limit to the ingredients you can use for brewing new concoctions. From basil to strawberry, from avocado to pomegranate, you have a wide range of options to choose from. Use any fruits, veggies or herbs you love and create your very own vitamin water.

Vitamin water is at its most beneficial when it is completely natural and free from additives or processing. The only way you can be sure it remains natural is if you make it yourself and as you will see in the second part of this book, it is very easy to make vitamin water at home even if you are not an expert in the culinary arts.

This gives you a great option to experiment with different flavors until you find the one you love. And while you are at it, you can treat your family and friends to tasty beverages that are completely healthy and the fruits of your labor. No more do you have to stock your fridge with cola and sports drinks.

It might be a good idea for you to add some sweetening to the natural vitamin water you make at home. Some fruits won't taste as sweet as they do in commercially available juice. In such drinks, companies use sugar and other ingredients to give the drink its taste. Hence, a little sweetener will help you drink almost any type of vitamin water you make.

At the end of the day, it comes down to whether or not you are willing to put in the effort to make natural vitamin water at home. With its endless customization options and ease of making, natural vitamin water may just be the perfect beverage for you. To help you start off on the right foot, 30 natural vitamin water recipes have been provided in the next part of this book.

HOMEMADE VS. STORE BOUGHT VITAMIN WATER

You might wonder why is it necessary for you to make natural vitamin water at home when you can easily find it in the market. There are many companies that have launched their own brands of vitamin water, each one featuring a range of flavors for you to choose from. They are backed with heavy advertising and tall claims that drinking the vitamin water might be the best solution to all your health issues.

As it turns out, there is little to separate commercial vitamin water from the other processed beverages you find in the market. Despite all the claims that the vitamin water is 'pure' and 'natural', research and tests have shown that it is nothing more than just fortified sugar. It doesn't take a rocket scientist to know that fortified sugar is bad for you.

However, the common perception remains that processed beverages deliver on their promises and are good for your health. This is not the case at all. By drinking commercially available vitamin water, all you end up with is rapid weight gain and a host of health problems in the future.

A major issue with branded vitamin water is that it isn't subject to the stringent laws applied to food products. As of now, the FDA has made it compulsory for the nutritional information of every food product to be mentioned on its packet or wrapper. Since vitamin water is marketed as a health product, there are no such requirements.

In fact, the reluctance of brands to own up to the farce has resulted in several controversies and scandals over the past few years. Even a company like Coca-Cola had to suffer backlash from advertisers when they tried to market vitamin water as healthy for the consumers in the UK.

As you can see, drinking commercially produced vitamin water might end up causing more harm than good. If you are concerned about your health and want to enjoy the benefits of natural vitamin water, you should make it at home. That way, you will be in complete control of the process from start to finish. There is no chance of fortified sugar entering the frame.

Not to forget that natural vitamin water made at home is incredibly healthy for you. We will look at the health benefits of homemade natural vitamin water in the next chapter.

HEALTH BENEFITS

The health benefits of vitamin water are numerous and varied. It is the ingredients of vitamin water that make it so beneficial for a person's health. In this chapter, we attempt to break down the health benefits, categorizing them according to the ingredients that deliver them.

The Fruits & Veggies

Fresh fruits and vegetables are loaded with nutrients. When they are processed to be added synthetically to vitamin water, their nutritional qualities decrease significantly. Since you are going to be using fresh fruits and veggies, you can gain immensely from the health benefits they provide.

Improves Digestion

Fruits and vegetables are full of fiber. Fiber is a key nutrient for your digestive health. Your digestive system depends on the quantity of fiber present in your system.

Drinking vitamin water ensures your fiber intake increases which will ultimately lead to an overall improvement in your digestive system.

Provides a Host of Nutrients

There is no doubt that fruits and vegetables are full of essential nutrients your body needs. As they are used in their natural and raw state, their nutrients remain intact when they are added to the water. This guarantees that your body receives all of the nutrients contained in the fruits and veggies that you added to the vitamin water.

Boosts Nutrient Absorption

Not only do the fruits and vegetables deliver a host of nutrients to your body, they also boost their absorption. Believe it or not, your body is well aware of the nutrients it receives. If they aren't natural, the body takes longer to absorb them, sometimes rejecting them completely. This isn't the case with homemade vitamin water as the nutrients are natural.

The Herbs

Like fruits and vegetables, herbs are also incredibly healthy when used in raw form. That is exactly the way they are added to vitamin water. As long as you are adding fresh herbs to your vitamin water, you can expect to enjoy the following health benefits.

Purifies Your Body

The foremost health benefit of consuming herbs, particularly rosemary, is that they purify your body. Once the herbs are in your system, they wage war on the free radicals and other harmful elements inside. As a result, your body is free from oxidative damage and a number of health problems are prevented.

Fights Blood Pressure and Diabetes

People suffering hypertension and/or diabetes will benefit hugely from consuming herbs regularly. Not only do they keep blood pressure in check, they also ensure your blood sugar levels hover around the normal mark.

Treats Common Infections

You can get rid of common infections like flu and cold by consuming herbs like mint and basil. Also, they are known to work wonders against irritable bowel syndrome (IBS). If you have been suffering from this digestive disorder, drinking vitamin water could be the easiest way to cure it.

<u>The Water</u>

It is no secret that drinking water is essential for us. Rather, most people should be drinking more water than they are at present. You need to have enough water in your system to keep it hydrated and flush out all the toxins and harmful elements. This is a common problem with people who drink too much soda or coffee in a day. They simply aren't thirsty enough to drink a sufficient amount of water.

Adding to the fact that you cannot survive without drinking water, there are several other health benefits of this substance you might consider boring. Water is a key ingredient in homemade vitamin water so drinking it regularly ensures your water intake increases. Here are some of the health benefits you can enjoy.

Minimizes Your Calorie Intake

The beverages that people drink in lieu of plain water, like sodas, coffee, juices, etc., are laced with caffeine and sugar. They also bring with them loads of calories. Once your calorie intake is on the rise, it becomes difficult for you to prevent weight gain. So, vitamin water is a great substitute for the calorie laden beverages you might otherwise be drinking.

Helps with Weight Loss

As mentioned above, your calorie intake decreases when you switch colas and processed juices for homemade vitamin water. Your weight is automatically under control from that moment onward. Also, the water your body gets through vitamin water will help break down the fat buildup in your body, further boosting your weight loss efforts.

Enhances Your Appearance

The effect of toxins and harmful elements inside your system takes no time to show up on your skin. If you are tired of blemishes, spots and acne, it is time you start drinking vitamin water. It will not only make your skin healthier but also more elastic. Not to mention the fact that your skin has to stay hydrated in order to look younger.

Fulfills Your Body's Needs

You may know that over 60% of the human body is made up of water. This is why your system relies on water to function properly. From digestion to circulation to the absorption of nutrients, each of these requires you to drink adequate quantities of water. When you drink vitamin water, your body's water needs are fulfilled.

Makes You Feel Better

Last, but not the least, dehydration cannot only cause physical health issues but also mood problems. You find it hard to feel comfortable and can easily get irritated when your body hasn't received enough water. Hence, drinking vitamin water regularly ensures your mood remains fine and you feel good all the time.

As you can see, there are numerous health benefits of drinking vitamin water. In addition, vitamin water is very simple to make as you will find out soon. There are no major risks involved in drinking vitamin water and neither are there any side effects. This makes drinking vitamin water a win-win solution.

BASICS OF MAKING VITAMIN WATER

Vitamin water is among the simplest recipes you can try at home. All you need to do is prepare the ingredients and put them in water. This is why it is such a great idea to try it at home. While we will go over the recipes for cocktails you can make at home, you need to know some basics of making vitamin water first.

Filtered Water

To enjoy the health benefits of vitamin water, it is imperative that the ingredients you use are pure and clean. Most importantly, the water you use for the recipes has to be filtered and purified. The main reason for this is the presence of certain harmful chemicals in regular tap water. They can create major health problems for you and you shouldn't risk using it.

Refilling

The ingredients for homemade vitamin water such as apples have skin that can be used in the drink to enhance its taste. Secondly, always make sure the fruits or vegetables are fresh. So when refilling your container of vitamin water, always make sure that you use fresh ingredients so you can gain maximum benefit.

Quantity

In the recipes listed below, you will find that specific quantities of the ingredients have been listed. The great thing about vitamin water is that there are few restrictions. The recipes are to be used as a guideline, not more. You can add as much or as little of the ingredients as you want. It depends on the kind of taste you are looking for in the vitamin water.

Size

The size of the pieces you cut the fruits and veggies into has a direct impact on the amount of nutrients that are passed on into the water.

In order to ensure maximum nutrients are part of the vitamin water you make, cut the fruits and veggies into bite size pieces or thin, long strips.

Sweetening

Sometimes, vitamin water does not taste the way you intend it to. If you want to sweeten the vitamin water you have made, stay away from commercial sugar. The best options are brown sugar and natural, unprocessed honey. This ensures the vitamin water tastes better without adding to its calorie count.

Essential Oils

Essential oils are an important part of maintaining overall good health, so why not pour some into your vitamin water? You only need to add a couple of drops of essential oils to the vitamin water to compound its health benefits. The natural goodness of the two combined will have a wonderful effect on your health.

Refrigeration

Once the vitamin water is ready, pour it into a pitcher or jar (more on them in the next chapter) and place it in the fridge. This allows time for the ingredients to mix perfectly with the water. Moreover, you get a chilled and cool drink.  This makes it a perfect beverage to make during summer.

These are some of the basics of making vitamin water. One thing you do need to keep in mind is that there is no right or wrong here. You can use several ingredients you come across at home. The idea is to mix fruits, vegetables and herbs with water to create a healthy and refreshing drink.

And don't forget that making vitamin water at home is supposed to be a fun-filled activity. Try to involve your kids in the process. Not only will you enjoy yourself but also enlighten them regarding the health benefits of vitamin water from an early age. Now that you know the basics of making vitamin water at home, it is time you understand the things you need for it.

Utensils & Ingredients

For all its health benefits and the hoopla surrounding it, vitamin water is surprisingly quite simple to make. As mentioned before, it is more convenient to make it at home than venture out to the store to get some. Before moving on to the recipes, it is important that you know the utensils and ingredients you are going to require for making vitamin water at home.

Fruits& Vegetables

First off, you need to have a steady stock of fresh fruits and vegetables. To make vitamin water, it is crucial that the fruits and veggies you use are fresh and ripe. There are no limitations on which ones you use.

Herbs

Complement the fruits and vegetables in your cocktail with herbs. Again, there is no limit on the type of herbs you use. You can either go with your personal preference or follow the instructions provided in the recipes in the next chapter. Herbs are an optional ingredient so you don't have to necessarily add them to the vitamin water if you do not prefer them.

Water

As mentioned in the previous chapter, you need to use filtered water for making vitamin water at home. Make sure there is plenty of purified water available to you so you can keep making vitamin water regularly.

Muddler or Knife

It depends on your preference whether you want to cut & slice the fruits and veggies or mash them to a pulp. Either way, they can be used for making vitamin water. However, it is better to cut the fruits and veggies for which you will need to have a sharp knife at hand. In some instances, you will also require a peeler. If you want to mash the ingredients, it is time you invest in a muddler or simply use a wooden spoon.

Jars/Pitchers

It is up to you whether you want to keep the vitamin water in a jar or a pitcher. The primary reason for this is to place the vitamin water in the fridge to cool it. Regardless of your choice, the ideal size for the container is 2 quarts.

Infusion Pitcher

Lastly, you can buy an infusion pitcher. This will allow you to make infused vitamin water, that is, the fruit will be strained from the water. This way, you can use the same ingredients for making multiple servings of vitamin water. You can also purchase an infusion water bottle to take with you to work or when you go for a jog or a run.

These are the basic utensils and ingredients you need for making vitamin water at home. Once again, you have to keep in mind that there are no restrictions whatsoever. As long as you are following the correct process for making vitamin water, you can use any ingredients and utensils you prefer. This brings us to the conclusion of the first part of this book. In Part 2, we will look at 30 amazing vitamin water recipes.

PART 2

Recipes

1. Apple-icious

Ingredients:

- 1 cup red apple, sliced
- 10 cups of water
- 1 cup green apple, sliced

Instructions:

1. Fill a pitcher with 10 cups of water
2. First add 1 cup sliced red apple
3. Next add 1 cup sliced green apple
4. Leave the mixture for a few minutes, so that all the nutrients are absorbed by the water

2. Exclusively Vanilla

Ingredients:

- 5 vanilla beans
- 8 cups of water
- 1 teaspoon vanilla extract
- 10 mint leaves

Instructions:

1. Fill a pitcher with 10 cups of water
2. Put in 5 vanilla beans and let stand for a few minutes, allowing the water to absorb the nutrients and taste
3. Next, add 1 teaspoon vanilla extract to the drink, and stir with a large plastic spoon
4. Throw in mint leaves, and refrigerate the drink for 8-12 hours

3. Fennel and Citrus

Ingredients:

- 2-3 grams fennel seeds, dried and crushed
- ½ cup boiling water
- 10 cups of water
- Juice of 2 lemons (do not discard the leftover lemons)
- 1 small orange, thinly sliced
- 12 fresh mint leaves, chopped

Instructions:

1. In advance, soak 2 to 3 grams fennel seeds in half a cup of boiling water for 8-10 minutes. Let the water cool down

2. In a pitcher, mix together 10 cups of water, lemon juice, the juiced lemons, orange slices, 12 chopped mint leaves and the mixture of fennel seeds and water

3. Stir with a large spoon, and refrigerate the drink for at least 8-10 hours before serving.

4. Strawberry and Lime

Ingredients:

- 6 strawberries
- 10 cups of water
- 1 lime, thinly sliced
- 12 fresh mint leaves, finely chopped

Instructions:

1. Take a pitcher and pour 10 cups of water in it
2. Next, throw in 6 strawberries, allowing the water to absorb the taste
3. Then add a thinly sliced lime, followed by 12 finely chopped mint leaves
4. Stir with a large plastic spoon
5. Your vitamin drink is ready, but you should store it in the refrigerator overnight to chill it before serving

5. Lemon and Cucumber

Ingredients:

- 1 cucumber
- 10 cups of water
- 1 lemon, thinly sliced
- ¼ cup fresh basil leaves, finely chopped
- 1/3 cup fresh mint leaves, finely chopped

Instructions:

1. In a pitcher, combine 10 cups of water with 1 cucumber and a thinly sliced lemon
2. Stir the contents of the jug with a large spoon, and then throw in ¼ cup of finely chopped mint leaves and 1/3 cup basil leaves
3. Refrigerate the pitcher for 8-10 hours and serve chilled

6. Ginger and Tea

Ingredients:

- 1 teaspoon ginger, ground
- 2 cups tea
- 10 cups of water
- 5 pieces ginger, cut into cubes

Instructions:

Here is a healthy alternative to tea!

1. Simply prepare 2 cups of tea the way you normally do, and heat 1 teaspoon of ground ginger in it
2. Take 10 cups of water in a pitcher pour 2 cups of ginger tea in it.
3. Add the ginger cubes to the solution, and stir with a large plastic spoon.
4. Leave it in the refrigerator overnight, and serve chilled.

7. Cinnamon and Apple

Ingredients:

- 1 cup apple, cut into cubes
- 10 cups of water
- 2 sticks of cinnamon
- 2 teaspoons cinnamon, ground

Instructions:

1. Taking a pitcher, pour 10 cups of water in it.
2. Next, add 1 cup of apple cubes into the water, allowing them to mix.
3. Then add 2 sticks of cinnamon, followed by 2 teaspoons of ground cinnamon.
4. Using a large spoon swirl the contents of the jug a few times and your traditional drink is ready.
5. But you need to refrigerate it 8-10 hours before serving.

36

8. Pineapple and Mint

Ingredients:

- 1 cup pineapple, cut into cubes
- 10 cups of water
- 12 fresh mint leaves, finely chopped

Instructions:

1. Pour 10 cups of water in a pitcher.
2. Add 1 cup of pineapple cubes into the water and let the water absorb the taste.
3. Using a large plastic spoon, stir the contents of the jug a few times, and add 12 finely chopped mint leaves to the mixture.
4. Refrigerate your exotic drink overnight, and serve chilled.

9. Lime, Mint and Berry

Ingredients:

- 7 strawberries
- 10 cups of water
- 1 lime, thinly sliced
- 12 fresh mint leaves, finely chopped

Instructions:

1. In a pitcher, pour 10 cups of water, followed by 7 strawberries.
2. After a few minutes, add thinly sliced lime, and stir with a large plastic spoon.
3. Add 12 finely chopped mint leaves to the jug, and you have created the perfect concoction for the spring season.
4. Place the pitcher in the refrigerator overnight and serve chilled.

10. Mango and Peach

Ingredients:

- 1 cup mango, cut into cubes
- 10 cups of water
- 1 cup peach, sliced

Instructions:

1. Take 10 cups of water in a pitcher
2. Add in cup of mango cubes, followed by 1 cup sliced peaches, allowing the water to absorb the nutrition and sweetness
3. Your sweet vitamin drink is ready, but you must refrigerate it overnight before serving

11. Pomegranate and Blueberry

Ingredients:

- ¼ cup pomegranate seeds
- 3 cups of water
- 5 fresh blueberries
- 4 fresh mint leaves, finely chopped

Instructions:

1. In a small pitcher or jar, pour 3 cups of water
2. Place ¼ cup pomegranate seeds in the pitcher, allowing the water to absorb the nutrients
3. Stir the water and seeds with a large plastic spoon, and cover the pitcher with a lid
4. You must refrigerate the vitamin drink for at least 8-10 hours before serving

12. Watermelon and Rosemary

Ingredients:

- 1 cup watermelon, cut into cubes
- 10 cups of water
- 2 stems rosemary

Instructions:

1. In a pitcher, combine 10 cups of water and 1 cup watermelon cubes, stirring the combination with a large plastic spoon

2. Next, add in 2 stems of rosemary, and your tasteful vitamin drink is ready

3. It is best served chilled, so refrigerate the drink for at least 8-10 hours before serving

13. Blackberry and Sage

Ingredients:

- 1 cup of blackberries, slightly crushed
- 10 cups of water
- 4 sage leaves

Instructions:

Here is a drink that is rich in antioxidants.

1. Firstly, pour 10 cups of water in a pitcher
2. Then place 1 cup crushed blackberries into the pitcher, letting them mix with the water
3. After stirring with a large spoon, throw in 4 sage leaves and your vitamin water is ready
4. But you should refrigerate it for 10-12 hours before serving

14. Ginger and Apple

Ingredients:

- 1 cup apple, cut into cubes
- 10 cups of water
- 3 pieces ginger, cut into cubes
- 1 teaspoon ginger, ground

Instructions:

1. Taking 10 cups of water in a pitcher, place 1 cup apple cubes in it

2. Leave for a few minutes to allow the water to absorb the nutrients

3. Next, add 3 pieces ginger, cubed, into the jug and 1 teaspoon ground ginger

4. Stir with a large plastic spoon, and place in the refrigerator for 8-12 hours before serving

15. Strawberry and Vanilla

Ingredients:

- 1 cup strawberries, sliced
- 8 cups of water
- 4 vanilla beans

Instructions:

1. In a pitcher, combine 8 cups of water and 1 cup sliced strawberries, and leave for a few minutes
2. Add 4 vanilla beans to the pitcher, and stir with a large plastic spoon
3. Refrigerate your vitamin supply overnight before serving

16. Coconut and Berries

Ingredients:

- 5 strawberries, sliced
- 8 cups of coconut water
- 1 cup mixed berries
- 1 grapefruit, peeled and sliced
- 3 mint leaves

Instructions:

1. In a small bowl, gently muddle strawberries, grapefruit and mixed berries together, just until they release their juices.

2. Fill a pitcher or jar with 8 cups of coconut water, and add the fruits and 3 mint leaves.

3. Let stand for a few minutes, and then stir with a large plastic spoon.

4. Refrigerate your vitamin drink for 8-10 hours before serving.

17. Basil and Berries

Ingredients:

- ½ cup basil leaves
- 8 cups of water
- 2 cups raspberries and blackberries (mixed)
- 12 sweet mint leaves

Instructions:

1. In a pitcher, pour 8 cups of water, and place 2 cups of berries in it
2. Let the mixture stand for a few minutes to let the water absorb the sweetness
3. Add ½ cup basil leaves and 12 sweet mint leaves, and stir with a large plastic spoon
4. Refrigerate the drink for 10-12 hours before serving. It tastes best after 1 day

18. Rose and Raspberry

Ingredients:

- 2 cups raspberries
- 4 cups of water
- ½ cup rose petals
- 2 drops of rose oil

Instructions:

1. Taking 4 cups of water in a small pitcher or jar, throw in 2 cups raspberries and ½ cup rose petals, letting the mixture stand for a few minutes
2. Next, add 2 drops of rose oil to the drink and stir with a large plastic spoon

19. Honeydew and Cantaloupe

Ingredients:

- 1 cup honeydew, cut into triangular wedges
- 8 cups of water
- 1 cup cantaloupe, cut into triangular wedges.
- 1 lime, thinly sliced

Instructions:

1. Place 8 cups of water in a pitcher
2. Add in 1 cup each of honeydew and cantaloupe, letting the mixture stand for a few minutes
3. Next, add lime slices, and stir the contents of the jug with a large plastic spoon

20. Pear and Cantaloupe

Ingredients:

- ½ cup pear, sliced
- 8 cups of water
- ½ cup cantaloupe

Instructions:

1. Place 8 cups of water in a pitcher
2. Throw in ½ cup pear slices and ½ cup cantaloupe slices, and let the mixture stand for a few minutes
3. Stir the contents of the jug with a large plastic spoon, cover with a lid and refrigerate overnight

This drink is best served chilled.

21. Kiwi and Strawberry

Ingredients:

- ¼ cup kiwi, sliced
- 8 cups of water
- 5 strawberries

Instructions:

1. Pour 8 cups of water in a pitcher
2. Place ¼ cup sliced kiwi and 5 strawberries, letting the mixture stand for a few minutes to let the water absorb the taste and nutrients
3. Cover the pitcher with a lid and place it in the refrigerator for 8-12 hours

The water tastes best after 12-24 hours

22. Peppermint and Grapefruit

Ingredients:

- 6 wedges grapefruit
- 8 cups of water
- 2 peppermint leaves

Instructions:

1. Fill a pitcher with 8 cups of water
2. Throw in 6 wedges of grapefruit in the water and let stand for a few minutes to allow the water to absorb the taste
3. Add 2 peppermint leaves to the mixture, and stir with a large plastic spoon
4. Refrigerate overnight before serving

23. Citrus Blast

Ingredients:

- 3 oranges
- 10 cups of cold water
- 2 lemons
- 1 lime
- 1 grapefruit
- 2 sprigs of thyme

Instructions:

1. Pour 10 cups of the cold water in a pitcher, and add 3 oranges to it
2. After a few minutes, add 2 lemons followed by a lime, 1 grapefruit and 2 sprigs of thyme
3. Shake the jug a few times, and place it in the refrigerator to chill for 8-10 hours

Recipes

24. *Immunity*

Ingredients:

- 3 oranges
- 10 cups of cold water
- 2 lemons
- 2 sprigs of sage
- 2 sprigs of thyme

Instructions:

1. Taking 10 cups of water in a pitcher throw in 3 oranges and leave for a few minutes
2. Next, add 2 lemons to the pitcher, and stir the mixture with a large plastic spoon
3. Refrigerate the drink for 8-10 hours, and you have a chilled fresh swig of immunity!

25. Pina Colada

Ingredients:

- ¼ cup fresh pineapple, chopped
- 2 teaspoons coconut milk
- 3 cups of water
- 1 fresh mint sprig
- 1 cucumber, thinly sliced
- 1 lime, thinly sliced
- 1/8 teaspoon sea salt

Instructions:

1. Combine water and coconut milk in a pitcher, and pour in 1/8 teaspoon sea salt
2. Add freshly chopped pineapple to the mixture, followed by a thinly sliced lime and cucumber
3. Before serving, throw in a fresh mint sprig, and refrigerate overnight

26. Very Berry

Ingredients:

- 5 fresh black cherries, pitted
- 2 cups of water
- ¼ cup mango, chopped
- ¼ cup peach, sliced

Instructions:

1. In a small pitcher, pour 2 cups of water and add 5 black cherries to it
2. After 5-10 minutes, add ¼ chopped mango and ¼ cup sliced peach to the pitcher, and cover it with a lid
3. Place the drink in the refrigerator for 8-12 hours, and serve chilled

27. Liquid Sunshine

Ingredients:

- ½ cup strawberries
- 4 cups of water
- ½ cup pineapple, sliced
- 1 cup pears, sliced
- 1 tablespoon wheatgrass
- 1/8 ounce borage oil
- 1 teaspoon raw cacao powder
- A pinch of salt

Instructions:

1. Crush the fruits together in a small bowl, and add this mixture to 4 cups of water and borage oil in a pitcher
2. Add salt to the mixture, followed by wheatgrass and raw cacao powder
3. Stir the mixture using a large plastic spoon, cover the pitcher and refrigerate it for 4-6 hours

28. Strictly Herbal

Ingredients:

- 10 cups of water
- ¼ cup fresh rosemary
- ¼ cup fresh mint

Instructions:

1. Muddle rosemary and mint together in a small bowl, and add this to an empty pitcher
2. Add 10 cups of water on top, letting it absorb the flavor
3. Cover the pitcher and refrigerate the drink overnight

Serve it chilled and you will taste the magic of herbs!

29. Mixed Bag

Ingredients:

- 1 cup pineapple, cut into cubes
- 10 cups of water
- 5 fresh black cherries, pitted
- ¼ cup peach, sliced
- ¼ cup fresh rosemary
- 10 mint leaves

Instructions:

1. Fill a pitcher with 10 cups of water
2. Place 1 cup pineapple cubes, 5 cherries and ¼ cup peach slices in the water and let stand for a few minutes
3. Add ¼ cup rosemary and 10 mint leaves on top, and stir with a large plastic spoon
4. Refrigerate the drink overnight, and serve chilled

Since this is a mixed bag drink, the choice of ingredients is entirely up to you.

30. Fruity Punch

Ingredients:

- ¼ cup peach, sliced
- 10 cups of water
- ¼ cup pineapple
- ¼ cup pears, sliced
- ¼ cup red cherries

Instructions:

1. Taking 10 cups of water in a pitcher, place ¼ cup peach slices in it
2. Follow this with ¼ cup pineapple, ¼ cup pear slices and ¼ cup red cherries
3. Let the mixture stand for a few minutes, so the various tastes and nutrients can mix
4. Stir the mixture with a large plastic spoon, cover with a lid and refrigerate for 8-12 hours

This drink is best served after 18-20 hours of preparation.

CONCLUSION

With this, we have come to the end of our book. As promised, we have told you everything you need to know about vitamin water, from its health benefits to its preparation. As you would know by now, making vitamin water is relatively easy. You simply need to collect the ingredients, prepare and throw them into a pitcher or jar.

You can start off with the 30 recipes we have provided you. That enables you to enjoy a different flavor of vitamin water every day of the month. All you have to do is read them and follow, and you will be happy with the result.

When it comes to vitamin water, there is just no limit on how many varieties you can have. It is like a laboratory experiment, where you can mix different ingredients together, the only difference being that there are no harmful effects, and you always end up with something tasteful and healthy.

Made in the USA
Lexington, KY
03 November 2013